PETER KENT'S
BIG BOOK OF
ARMOR

KINGFISHER
LONDON & NEW YORK

Illustrations by Peter Kent

Distributed in the U.S. by Macmillan,
175 Fifth Ave., New York, NY 10010
Distributed in Canada by H.B. Fenn and Company Ltd.,
34 Nixon Road, Bolton, Ontario L7E 1W2

Library of Congress Cataloging-in-Publication data
has been applied for.

ISBN: 978-0-7534-6423-6

Kingfisher books are available for special
promotions and premiums. For details contact:
Special Markets Department, Macmillan,
175 Fifth Avenue, New York, NY 10010.

For more information, please visit
www.kingfisherbooks.com

Picture credit: p. 6–7 Shutterstock/mehmetsait

Printed in China
10 9 8 7 6 5 4 3 2 1
1TR/0410/WKT/UNT/157MA/C

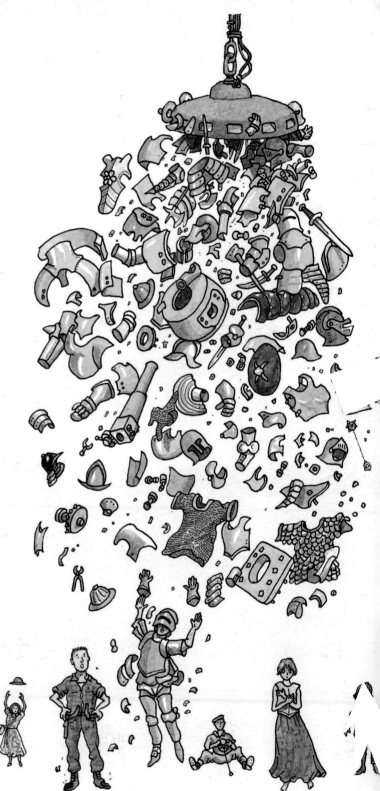

Note to readers: The website addresses listed in this book are
correct at the time of going to print. However, due to the
ever-changing nature of the Internet, website addresses and
content can change. Websites can contain links that are
unsuitable for children. The publisher cannot be held
responsible for changes in website addresses or content or
for information obtained through a third party. We strongly
advise that Internet searches be supervised by an adult.

Contents

INTRODUCTION

When most people think of armor, they imagine a clanking suit of armor, the type of clothing worn by a man whose tailor is a blacksmith—but there is more to it than that. Armor is defensive covering, something that protects the wearer from harm, but not just during war. There are many more dangers to people than battle-axes, bullets, and bombs. Most people put on some kind of armor every day, whether it's a bicycle helmet, shin guards, or safety goggles. And it's not just people that wear it—just look at a tortoise or the aptly named armadillo. Whenever something needs protection, there you'll find armor. From a battleship to a beetle, there's nothing like armor to keep it safe.

Hard plastic knee and elbow pads with a helmet keep this scooter rider safe. They were unknown 30 years ago when grazed knees were universal.

Legs are in danger during a game of soccer, with all those cleats hacking at the ball. Guards save shins from cuts and bruises.

The shining knight in a polished suit on his equally well-protected horse is most people's idea of what armor looks like.

Carpentry can be lethal, too. Safety requires a pair of acoustic earmuffs, safety goggles, and a face mask.

The kitchen can be a dangerous place. An apron and oven mitts protect the cook from spitting fat and hot baking sheets.

Strange concrete objects such as this are part of the sea coast's armor, defending it against strong waves.

Soldiers long dreamed of armored vehicles to keep them safe on the battlefield. This armored war cart was used by Hussites from Bohemia in the 1400s.

Construction sites can be almost as dangerous as battlefields, so workers wear helmets and steel-toed boots.

SPF-50 sunblock acts as invisible armor, filtering out the harmful ultraviolet rays in sunlight.

A helmet with a visor to protect his eyes against a toxic spray is standard wear for today's security guard.

Animals have worn armor since long before there were humans. The hard plates covering an armadillo protect it against predators' teeth and claws.

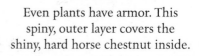

Even plants have armor. This spiny, outer layer covers the shiny, hard horse chestnut inside.

Insects live inside a complete suit of armor because they have their skeleton on the outside. The hard outer casing is, for their size, very strong.

EARTH'S ARMOR

The atmosphere is an envelope of gases that surrounds Earth—without it, no life would be possible. As Earth moves through space, the atmosphere acts both as a shield, giving protection from most of the deadly rays and meteorites that continually bombard us, and as a container, stopping the air from escaping into space.

The atmosphere, which is around 430 mi. (700km) thick, does not work like a normal sheet of armor—lumps of rock do not simply bounce off it. A solid object piercing the atmosphere creates friction as its surface drags through the air, and more speed means more friction and more heat. Meteors may burn up entirely, or else only small fragments reach the ground as meteorites. Only the very biggest meteor or asteroid could pass through the atmosphere in one large piece. The atmosphere also acts as a filter to radiation, only letting through sunlight, heat, and some less harmful rays.

The exosphere is the very top layer. It starts about 400 mi. (650km) above Earth and finally merges into space at about 5,000 mi. (8,000km).

Solar shield

Most meteors burn up in the mesosphere about 40–50 mi. (60–80km) above Earth, where the air is thick enough to cause friction.

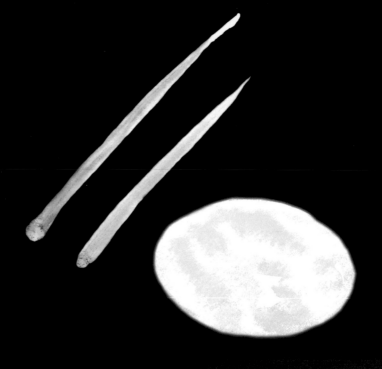

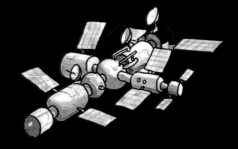

Although it is made of nothing but gas, the atmosphere is incredibly heavy, weighing about 5,500 trillion tons.

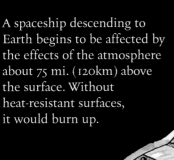

A spaceship descending to Earth begins to be affected by the effects of the atmosphere about 75 mi. (120km) above the surface. Without heat-resistant surfaces, it would burn up.

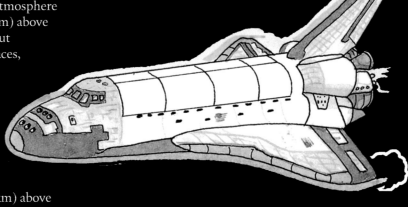

About 50 mi. (85km) above Earth, the ionosphere absorbs much of the ultraviolet light. Cosmic rays and gamma rays are also neutralized there.

One way of coping with global warming would be to create artificial solar shields to reflect the Sun's rays back into space, similar to a windshield screen that prevents the inside of a car from getting too hot.

Solar shield

The vital part of the stratosphere is the ozone layer, about 9–22 mi. (15–35km) above Earth. This filters out ultraviolet light.

The lowest layer of the atmosphere is the troposphere. About 80 percent of all the gases in the atmosphere are in this layer. This is where oxygen is the thickest and also where the final filtering of harmful rays takes place.

COASTAL DEFENSE

When you are walking on a beach or scrambling up cliffs, you are playing on the gigantic suit of armor that protects the land in its never-ending battle with the sea. There are natural defenses against the waves: hard (such as cliffs) and soft (such as sand dunes), but still the coast is washed away. Ever since people began to live by the sea, they have been defending their homes and harbors against waves. The Romans were the first to build breakwaters, but it was the Dutch who started building sea defenses on a large scale. For the Netherlands and other countries that lie below sea level, sea defenses are vital armor.

Gabions are a way of making "large rocks" by scooping up smaller rocks and packing them in boxes made of wire mesh.

This sea wall has a slope at the bottom to make the waves break and a curved top to deflect the force back.

Wooden revetments are easily damaged by waves and need constant repair. They are unpopular because they stop people from getting to the water.

CONCRETE BLOCKS

Interlocking concrete shapes make a great sea defense. These are made according to many different designs, but the most common is the "dolos." The legs lock together so that they form an immovable barrier, while the spaces in between allow the water to wash through and lose most of its energy.

X-bloc

Accropod

Tetrapod

A-jack

Dolos

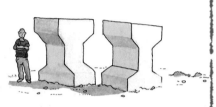

Akmon

A.D. 200 The great harbor of Ostia was the main port for ancient Rome. The outer harbor with its curved breakwaters and lighthouse created a safe place for ships to anchor.

ANIMAL ARMOR

Millions of years before there were human designers of armor, nature had evolved the basic ways of providing body protection—because almost every animal has an enemy that wants to kill it. An animal without any defense is soon extinct. The best defense is to run away or hide, but for those that can't, nature has provided armor in the form of shells, scales, and thick skins. The more dangerous an animal's enemies are, the more complete its armor has to be.

HORNS

The basic forms of weapons are clubs that crush, spears that stab, and swords that cut. The horns of animals are the equivalent of spears. Horns and tusks, animals' natural defenses, are sought by poachers, endangering many species.

Rhinoceros

Moose

TEETH

Animals' teeth are designed to cut and tear. The terrible fangs of Tyrannosaurus rex and the modern-day tiger's huge canines are the classic weapons of the predator.

Narwhal

Tiger

Crocodile

Tyrannosaurus rex

NATURAL ARMOR

The strongest form of armor is a shell. Its continuous surface can resist heavy blows, but it is heavy and restricts movement. The most flexible form of armor is a strong hide like that of an elephant or a hippopotamus—but in order to be effective, it must be very thick.

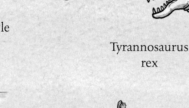

Turtle

Cone shell

Conch shell

Ladybug

Elephant

Hippopotamus

A coat of bony plates or scales is easier to move in. It is strong but there are weak places in the joints.

Pangolin

Ankylosaurus

CLAWS

The paw of a grizzly bear is like a spiked club. The crab's claws and the golden eagle's talons are used to crush and grip their prey.

Bear

Crab

Golden eagle

BEAKS

Birds' beaks have many uses: the macaw's cracks open nuts; the woodpecker's chisels wood; the heron's spears fish; and the vulture's tears its prey.

Macaw

Woodpecker

Heron

Vulture

PLANT ARMOR

Most of the world's creatures are vegetarians and, in order to survive, plants have evolved ways to protect themselves. Trees need a hard, outer layer to protect the growing wood inside, and seeds need a case to protect them long enough for them to ripen. But these defenses cannot be too good. Plants need to be eaten—if their armor were completely effective, animals would be unable to feed and would starve.

Bark protects the tree against the cold, keeps in moisture, keeps out insects, and prevents injuries. It is continually renewed from within as the inner bark dies.

The seeds of the Bhutan pine are inside this pinecone made up of woody plates.

The bark of the cork tree can be more than 3 ft. (1m) thick. It is harvested mostly to provide the corks used to seal wine bottles.

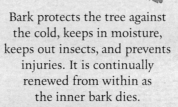

The hard cases of seeds are the most common form of plant armor. The horse chestnut seed has a spiky shell. In the U.K. and Ireland, these seeds are strung and bashed together in a popular children's game.

The pinecone of the cluster pine is made of woody scales reinforced with sharp prickles.

Because coconut trees are very tall, their seedcases need to be very strong in order to avoid breaking when they hit the ground.

PRIMITIVE PROTECTION

20,000 B.C. All basic armor must defend against stabbing and blows to the head.

The first pieces of human armor were made from natural materials: shields were formed from woven twigs, wood, or animal hide, and body armor used the natural toughness of skins and hides. Other primitive armor was made from hoops of wood, strips of bark, slats of wood or bone sewn into fabric, and rope woven into a stiff suit. Some shields and helmets were made from tortoise shells. All these "green" forms of armor were no longer used as soon as metal was easily available.

A.D. 1890 The first armor was probably like this Dayak armor from Borneo, made of goat hides.

1850 This Inuit man wears a breastplate of walrus tusk plates laced together with rawhide.

1800 On the South Pacific Islands, strong armor was made from coconut fiber rope and woven cane.

1780 Wood bent into hoops and covered in hide made armor for Chukchi warriors from Siberia.

1400 The Aztecs wore very effective armor of padded linen. Knights wore suits to make them look like jaguars or eagles.

ANCIENT ARMOR

I t was in Egypt, the Middle East, and China that civilization in cities and states first appeared. Disagreements between them led to fighting on a large scale, with well-organized armies, but it was the discovery of metal—first copper, then bronze, and finally iron—that truly revolutionized warfare. Metal weapons cut with deadly efficiency, so more protection became necessary. The first armor was made of leather and thick cloth, sometimes reinforced with small metal plates.

1275 B.C. In ancient Egypt, only the pharaoh could afford a coat of bronze plates sewn on leather; soldiers wore armor of thick leather, hippopotamus hide, or padded linen.

1020 B.C. The Bible says that the giant Philistine Goliath wore armor made of brass, but it was more likely to have been bronze.

3000 B.C. The first Egyptian soldiers fought savage tribes armed with only primitive weapons. They did not need to wear armor, and they carried only large cowhide shields.

900 B.C. These strange decorated bronze helmets were worn more for show than for serious fighting.

2500 B.C. Sumerians wore long, thick leather cloaks strengthened with bronze disks in the same way that their wooden shields were strengthened. Their helmets were made of leather or copper.

750 B.C. Assyrians wore armor made of bronze scales laced together, plus a well-designed helmet with cheek pieces.

1300 B.C. The Hittites were the first to use iron swords and helmets.

CLASSICAL ARMOR

The most beautiful and elegant armor was made by the ancient Greeks. Armor was so important to them that they even had a god, Hephaistos, dedicated to metalwork. A few centuries later, Rome was the greatest power in the Western world. The Roman Empire, stretching from the Arabian desert to the far north of Britain, was defended by an excellent professional army.

1200 B.C. During the siege of Troy, warriors wore helmets made of boar tusks and carried huge cowhide shields.

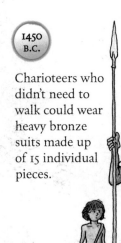

1450 B.C. Charioteers who didn't need to walk could wear heavy bronze suits made up of 15 individual pieces.

490 B.C. Greek foot soldiers, or hoplites, wore bronze or leather body armor with bronze helmets and bronze greaves on their legs.

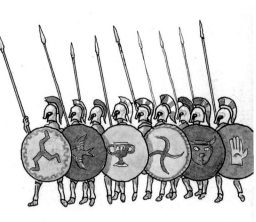

420 B.C. Greek hoplites formed a solid mass called a phalanx. Each man was protected by a large shield and carried a long spear.

GREEK HELMETS

Greek helmets were beautifully shaped and skillfully made by hammering out a single sheet of bronze. Each city had its own distinctively shaped helmet.

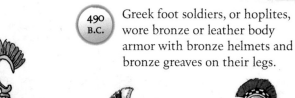

Illyrian helmet   Spartan helmet   Corinthian helmet

Chalcidian helmet   Boeotian helmet   Thracian helmet

CELTIC WARRIORS

Most of the Romans' Celtic enemies wore no armor—and some even fought naked. No wonder the Romans almost always won!

A.D. 100 Roman soldiers, or legionaries, wore a standardized armor of metal plates with a helmet that defended the cheeks and neck. An apron of metal disks gave extra protection.

A.D. 35 Flexible plate armor was introduced during the reign of the Roman emperor Tiberius. The plates were an effective defense and were also light and easy to wear.

55 B.C. Legionaries in Caesar's time wore a chain-mail shirt and a bronze helmet. Officers wore a bronze cuirass that mimicked the muscles of the abdomen.

A.D. 100 Rectangular shields could be formed into a *testudo*, or tortoise, to make an instant and very effective "tank." It was used to attack walls and ramparts while under heavy bombardment.

15

MEDIEVAL ARMOR

When the last Roman emperor was deposed in A.D. 476, Europe entered a period known as the Dark Ages. The continent splintered into a chaos of warring barbarian tribes. The peoples that replaced the Romans—the Saxons, Franks, Goths, Vandals, and Lombards—were brave and fierce but not very advanced in military technology. They thought that the Romans' armor made of metal plates was too complicated. The barbarian kings, nobles, and warriors wore chain-mail shirts and richly decorated helmets. Common soldiers had to make do with leather jerkins.

A.D. 400

The Saxons were named after their saxes (long knives) and the Lombards after their long axes.

750

This noble is wearing a magnificent helmet decorated with gold. Most helmets of the Dark Ages are known as *spagenhelm*.

1120

The crusaders wore linen surcoats to protect them from the fierce heat. Their great battle helmets were very uncomfortable and very difficult to see out of.

1400

Common soldiers wore leather jerkins called jacks. They were often strengthened with small plates of metal or horn. Their helmets were known as pots.

1400

Every knight needed a squire and a couple of servants to help him dress and to keep his armor clean.

16

1200
Suits of armor were still mainly made of chain mail, but plates of boiled leather were added to vulnerable parts.

1350
This is typical armor of the Hundred Years' War, with metal plates added to the chain mail. The wasp-waist look was very fashionable.

1500
A good horse was expensive and needed protection: a knight didn't want it to be killed under him, or else he would have to fight on foot.

1450
By the 1400s, knights wore a suit made completely of plate armor, weighing about 80 lbs. (35kg).

800
The Vikings never wore helmets with horns. They did have helmets that looked like they were wearing glasses, but the nose-bar helmet was more common.

1066
The Normans wore chain-mail shirts and helmets like the Vikings but also added kite shields. These protected the legs as well as the body.

MAKING ARMOR

Armorers were the most famous and best-paid craftsmen in the Middle Ages. The best armor was made in Germany and Italy. Learning the skill of making complicated armor by hand took four years as an apprentice and then another four years as a paid workman. After passing an examination by making a special piece—his masterpiece—the workman became a master. Armorers joined to form a guild, which set prices and inspected work to make sure it was of the highest quality.

1 The master armorer took the order, measured the client, and discussed what he wanted. Some clients left wax models of their limbs with their armorer so that he could make replacements without needing to see them again.

2 A bar of wrought iron or soft steel was hammered flat, at first by a water-powered hammer and then by hand.

3 This reduced the bar to a thin sheet about 0.15 in. (4mm) thick.

4 The metal was cut into flat shapes with shears, following a pattern.

5 The parts were hammered into shape on a wooden mold. This was the most skilled part of the entire process.

6 The parts were heated in a furnace to harden the surface. Every armorer had a secret recipe for this process. One smeared the surface of the metal with rancid pork lard and wrapped it in a goat hide covered in clay.

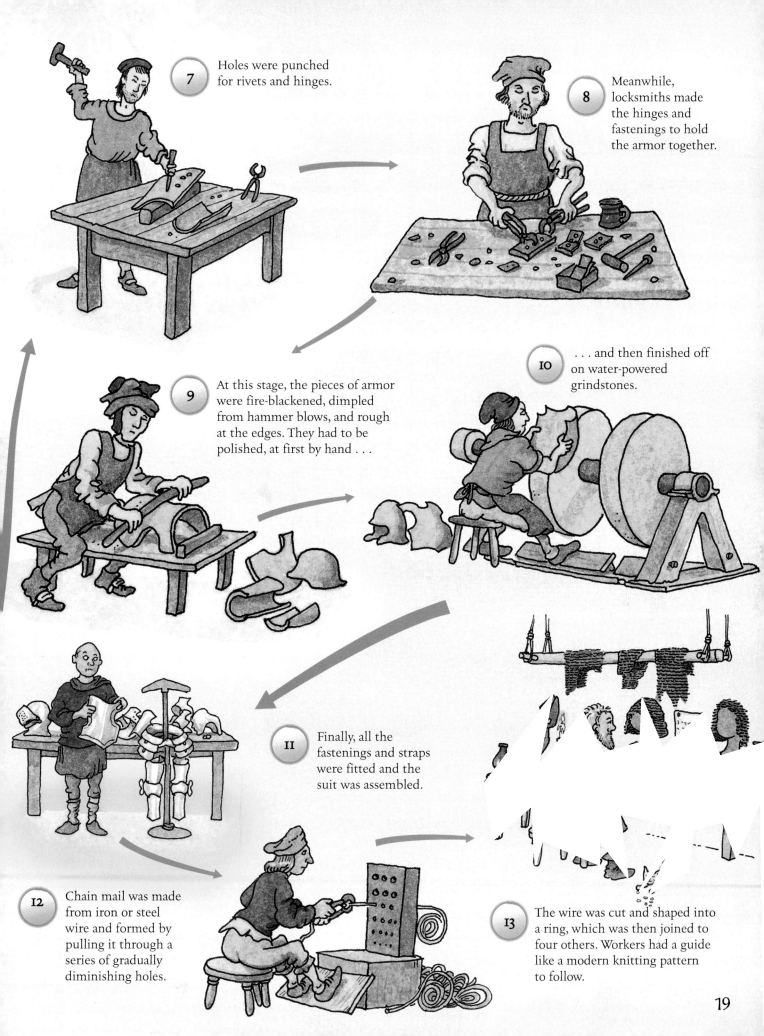

7 Holes were punched for rivets and hinges.

8 Meanwhile, locksmiths made the hinges and fastenings to hold the armor together.

9 At this stage, the pieces of armor were fire-blackened, dimpled from hammer blows, and rough at the edges. They had to be polished, at first by hand . . .

10 . . . and then finished off on water-powered grindstones.

11 Finally, all the fastenings and straps were fitted and the suit was assembled.

12 Chain mail was made from iron or steel wire and formed by pulling it through a series of gradually diminishing holes.

13 The wire was cut and shaped into a ring, which was then joined to four others. Workers had a guide like a modern knitting pattern to follow.

BLOODY BATTLES

Medieval battles were dreadful, confusing, bloody affairs. Once the fighting began, the commanders had no control over their armies. They could not send messages, and even if they did, their soldiers would not have heard them above the din of thousands of men yelling and the clanging of weapons on armor. It must have sounded like a football game in which every spectator was banging a metal bucket with a poker and shouting, too.

The fighting did not last long. No man was strong and fit enough to fight for hours wearing armor and wielding a heavy weapon. Usually one army charged, and there was a struggle until one side or the other turned and ran. Medieval soldiers only took prisoners who were noble and could pay a ransom to buy their freedom.

FIGHTING FOR FUN

Tournaments or mock battles were, along with hunting, the sport of knights. They began in the 1100s as one-on-one combats and then developed into mock battles, called melees, that were so dangerous that many knights were killed. A safer sport was devised in which two knights rode toward each other, trying to unhorse one another or score points by hitting each other's shields.

A tournament was the chance for a knight to show off all his martial skills before an admiring crowd of noble ladies: the applause of common peasants was of no account, assuming they were allowed to watch the event in the first place. A tournament looked and sounded thrillingly warlike, but in reality it was no more dangerous than a game of football.

21

Asian Armor

India was often invaded from the north by armies of horsemen, so cavalry (soldiers who fought on horseback) became the most important part of Indian armies. The last invaders were the Muslim Moguls who set up an empire in Delhi.

Indian soldiers wore suits of chain mail and helmets richly decorated with gold and brass. Plates of iron were added to the body and arms. Helmets were conical and pointed, like the roofs of mosques, and had adjustable nose guards. Horses and elephants were armored, too.

Japanese warriors, or samurai, were like the medieval knights of Europe in spirit, but their armor was very different. It was lighter and more flexible than European armor, designed to absorb the shock of a blow rather than to break it. A suit of armor was made of hundreds of thin strips of steel laced together with silk threads. The Japanese seemed deliberately to make their armor as complicated as possible. Each suit had dozens of parts with many different names for each of them, and there are more types of Japanese chain mail than there are from all of the rest of the world combined.

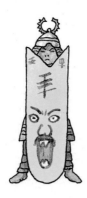

A.D. 1300 As well as iron, Chinese armor was made from bronze, leather, wicker, and even paper.

1640 Swallow-tailed shields were popular. This archer wears a leather coat studded with steel plates.

1400 Dogs and other animals carrying fire bombs were used to spread confusion among the enemy.

1100 The impressive armor of this heavy cavalryman and his horse is made of bronze scales.

1400 Thin strips of steel laced together were called lamellar armor. It was always light and flexible.

1600 More modern Japanese armor was made from larger steel plates and was much less complicated.

210 B.C. The figures in the Terracotta Army are exact life-size models of ancient Chinese soldiers, such as this one.

Japanese helmets

Japanese helmets came in a wide range of shapes. Fierce face masks were worn to frighten the enemy as well as for protection.

1640 This soldier's armor is very simple and cheap. The string of bags around his neck contain rice.

ARMOR IN DECLINE

As soon as handguns became widely used, armor became increasingly unpopular. It had to be made thicker in order to stop bullets, which made it too heavy and uncomfortable to wear. Ordinary soldiers refused to wear armor unless they were paid extra and were not made to march more than 10 mi. (16km) per day.

It was not just guns—crossbows could also pierce armor plates—but a powerful combination of new infantry tactics and new weaponry that made the knight obsolete. Swiss, German, and Czech infantry learned to fight in giant squares bristling with lances, similar to the Greek phalanx. In the square were handgunners and crossbowmen who, safe among the spears that kept the attacking cavalry at bay, picked off the riders.

By the middle of the 1500s, armor, particularly for the infantry, was reduced to a helmet, a breastplate, and a backplate with thigh protection. Men armed with muskets did not usually bother with body armor. It got in the way when they were firing and was an extra weight to carry, added to that of their heavy gun.

A.D. 1670 Kings and generals still wore a suit of armor for their portraits, as it made them look stern and warlike.

1848 Engineers digging trenches close to a fortress wore heavy helmets all the way into the 1800s.

1520 German mercenary

1560 Polish officer

1600 Pikeman

1645 A Roundhead cavalry trooper of the English Civil War.

1798 Armor finally shrank to nothing more than the small steel plate at this officer's throat.

1760 Prussian cavalry wore breastplates and backplates, heavy boots, and a hat reinforced with iron.

1861 A few officers in the American Civil War wore steel breastplates disguised as uniform vests.

1815 The armor of the French cuirassiers was not much use against cannons at the Battle of Waterloo.

25

ARMOR MAKES A COMEBACK

uring World War I, many soldiers died of head wounds, and it was soon realized that a steel helmet could save lives. The French army was the first to issue them in 1915, and all other armies soon followed. Body armor was designed, too, but it was too heavy to use comfortably. During World War II, all soldiers wore helmets, but body armor was only used by bomber crews. Because the men were sitting or lying down, weight was not a problem.

A.D. 1918 German body armor was very heavy and worn only by soldiers guarding dangerous places.

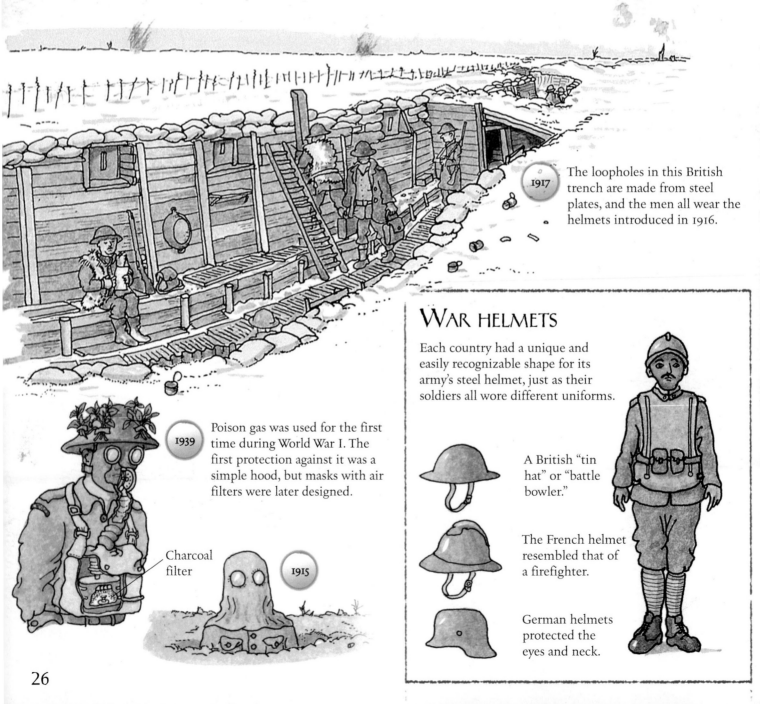

1917 The loopholes in this British trench are made from steel plates, and the men all wear the helmets introduced in 1916.

1939 Poison gas was used for the first time during World War I. The first protection against it was a simple hood, but masks with air filters were later designed.

Charcoal filter

1915

WAR HELMETS

Each country had a unique and easily recognizable shape for its army's steel helmet, just as their soldiers all wore different uniforms.

A British "tin hat" or "battle bowler."

The French helmet resembled that of a firefighter.

German helmets protected the eyes and neck.

1918 Sailors wore gloves and hoods of flameproof fabric to protect them from the flash of an explosion.

1916 These Austrian messenger dogs wearing hoods are safe from toxic gas.

1917 This British body armor consisted of a metal plate inside felt lining, with padding behind it.

1944 Gunners in American bombers wore a steel helmet and full body armor. Headphones in the helmet allowed communication with the pilot.

1940 This set of armor included a spade on the chest for extra protection and steel goggles.

1940 Bomb-aimers lay flat on the floor of the aircraft and often made improvised body armor from the hubcap of a car.

1969 Rioters in Northern Ireland threw rocks at the soldiers' unprotected ankles. They responded with armor made from baked-bean cans.

27

MODERN ARMOR

If a knight time-traveled from 1400 to 1900, he would have been surprised and alarmed to see that soldiers no longer wore armor. Then, if he were to resume his time travel forward another 100 years, he would be amazed to see soldiers in armor that looked remarkably like his. Armor, made from lighter materials than steel, staged a big comeback in the late 20th century. From soldiers and police to security guards, everyone is wearing it now.

Medieval and modern soldiers look similar in their helmets and body armor, except that the materials are different.

Riot police wear helmets with plastic visors, body armor, and flameproof coveralls. Their shields are made of clear, high-impact plastic.

Police and guards at checkpoints carry mini shields in the form of bullet-proof clipboards.

Even limited-duty police officers, such as community service or community safety officers, often wear knifeproof vests, just in case.

U.S. soldiers in the Vietnam War were the first in modern times to wear armor in battle.

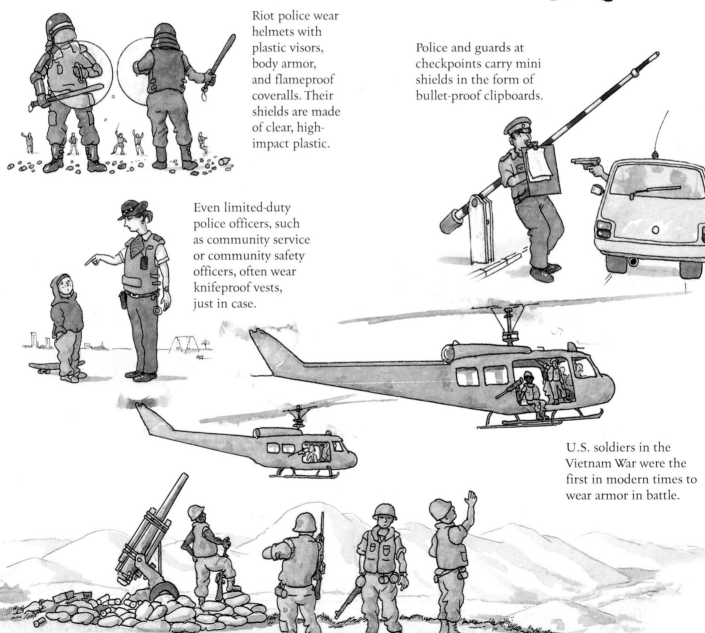

A massive frontal plate and a helmet with a thick plexiglass visor protect bomb-disposal experts. The suit is made of a tough, flameproof plastic fiber.

The most up-to-date armor for riot police is made almost entirely from hard plastic plates. It is designed to protect against stones and glass bottles but not bullets.

The most modern body armor is made from Kevlar and ceramic plates and is fastened with Velcro.

The armor of the future will be as light and easy to wear as regular clothes but as tough as steel.

Ballistic nylon, 0.3 in. (7mm) thick

Padded lining

Camouflage coating

A modern combat helmet

Ceramic plate

Kevlar fabric

Velcro fasteners

Modern body armor

ATHLETIC ARMOR

All popular sports have an element of danger, and some people love the adrenalin rush. For them, a game with hard balls thrown at great speed is always going to be more exciting than golf; ice hockey is more exhilarating than showjumping; and it is a boring car race that does not have at least one crash. But even the most daring athlete needs some protection . . .

A.D. 150 In ancient Rome, there were many types of gladiators, each with a specific style of armor and weapons. Two similar gladiators never fought each other. The crowd liked to see two different types, pitting their individual skills against each other.

1400 The Aztecs wore padding on their elbows and waists to play a fast and dangerous game with a solid rubber ball.

Motorcyclists wear helmets and suits of leather and Kevlar with high-impact plastic inserts to protect their knees, elbows, shoulders, and backs.

Fencers wear face masks of stainless steel and a jacket made of tightly woven nylon.

The puck in ice hockey is hard and travels very fast. The goalkeeper is padded and protected like a medieval knight.

During the Middle Ages, hunting dogs often wore leather armor with metal studs to protect them from wild boars' tusks.

A fastball pitch in baseball can reach 100 mph (160km/h). Cricket is a similar sport, in which a ball is hit by a cricket bat. In both sports, it is crucial that the players wear protective gear.

Football players wear helmets with face masks and elaborate body armor with shoulder pads to absorb the shocks of the game.

In the past, soccer goalkeepers wore helmets to protect their heads against players' kicks.

INDUSTRIAL ARMOR

Industry has always been dangerous. Workers are threatened by extreme heat, poisonous fumes, and falling objects. In the past 50 years, even deadlier jobs have been created. The crew members of some rockets handle fuel that could dissolve them; a nuclear reactor is lethally radioactive. Specialized clothing now protects most workers in dangerous jobs. This is just as much armor as the metal suit of the knight. If there is a gap in the protection, the result is just as deadly.

Miners' helmets are made of metal, fiberglass, or plastic and are usually equipped with a light.

Workers cutting fish or meat wear chain-mail gloves and aprons as well as arm guards.

Gloves made of Kevlar are used by workers where there is a danger of cuts or piercing.

In the 1800s, shining brass helmets were popular with firefighters in some countries, but they were too heavy and too tall to be practical.

Welders must wear a darkly tinted glass mask to protect their eyes from the intense heat and light.

Workers in foundries, who deal with hot metal, need flameproof hoods and aprons, thick gloves, and reinforced boots.

This inflatable radiation suit (above, left) was made by a tire manufacturer. Sealed suits are used wherever there is radioactivity (above, right).

SAFETY SUITS

Space and the depths of the sea are dangerous. In space, it is extremely cold, and full of deadly cosmic rays, whizzing rocks, and specks of space dust. The deep sea, too, is freezing and the pressure of the water increases with depth. To walk in space, you must have a very special suit, and the only way to dive comfortably in deep water is to wear armored diving equipment. At 200 ft. (60m) down, the pressure of the water is five times greater than at the surface, so a diving suit must be very strong in order to resist it.

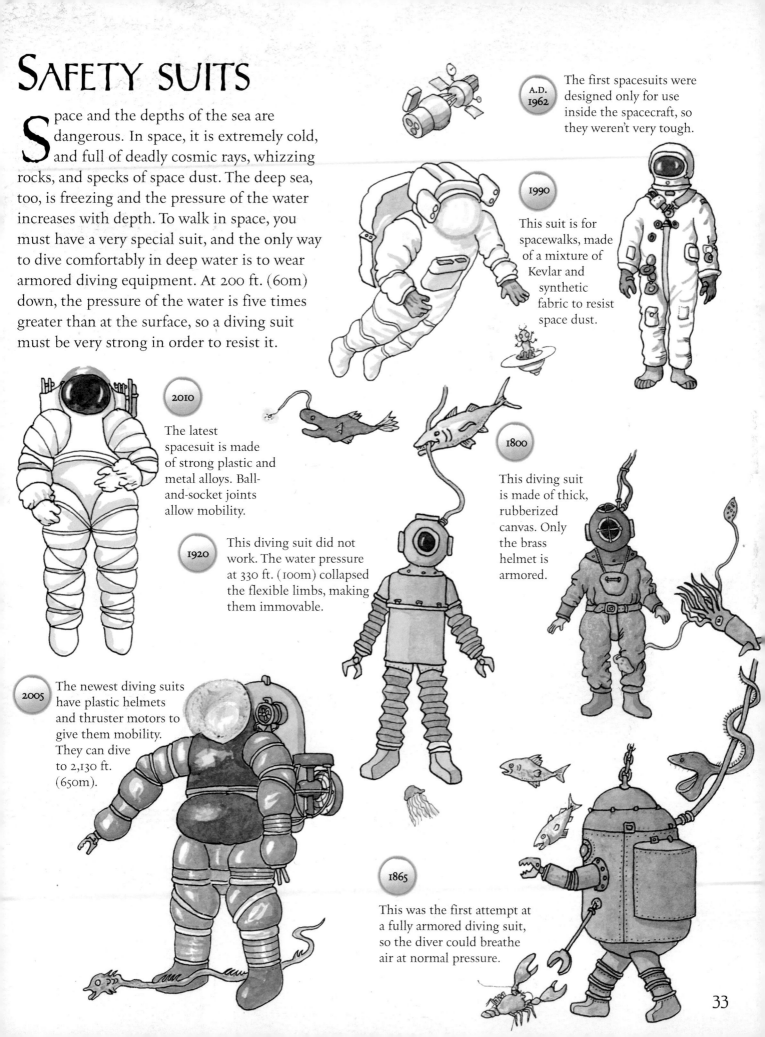

A.D. 1962
The first spacesuits were designed only for use inside the spacecraft, so they weren't very tough.

1990
This suit is for spacewalks, made of a mixture of Kevlar and synthetic fabric to resist space dust.

2010
The latest spacesuit is made of strong plastic and metal alloys. Ball-and-socket joints allow mobility.

1920
This diving suit did not work. The water pressure at 330 ft. (100m) collapsed the flexible limbs, making them immovable.

1800
This diving suit is made of thick, rubberized canvas. Only the brass helmet is armored.

2005
The newest diving suits have plastic helmets and thruster motors to give them mobility. They can dive to 2,130 ft. (650m).

1865
This was the first attempt at a fully armored diving suit, so the diver could breathe air at normal pressure.

33

WAR WAGONS

Soldiers have dreamed of war chariots or armored carts that could move around the battlefield since ancient times. The problem was always how to power them. Men weren't strong enough, and horses pulling from outside could be killed. Horses inside took up too much room, and they weren't powerful enough to move a heavy vehicle over rough ground. It wasn't until the invention of small, powerful engines 120 years ago that a true armored fighting vehicle became possible.

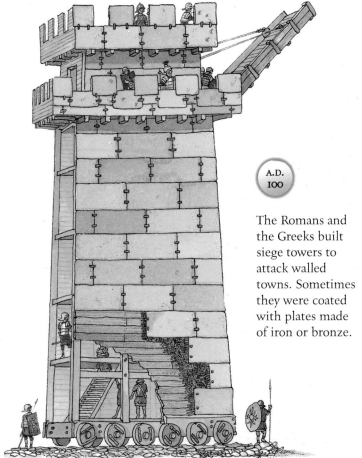

A.D. 100

The Romans and the Greeks built siege towers to attack walled towns. Sometimes they were coated with plates made of iron or bronze.

900 B.C.

This battering ram was used by the Assyrians to attack cities. It was protected by leather skins, and the sides were made of wicker, like a basket.

1425

The Hussite armies in what is now the Czech Republic would draw their war carts in a circle and chain them together to make a fortress. The carts mounted many small guns, and they always defeated the knights who attacked them.

1300

This was a common sight at a siege during the Middle Ages. The battering ram hung from the roof of a shed on wheels, which was protected by strong boards covered in animal hides.

c. 1500 Leonardo da Vinci was a great inventor as well as an artist. He drew plans for this circular war vehicle that was powered by men turning crank handles inside. It was never built, though.

1530 If you ignore the fancy costume, this is actually a sensible siege tower. It moved forward on skids by winching itself on a pulley attached to a strong post.

1560 Guido Ramelli designed this ingenious amphibious armored car. It was powered by four men turning the paddle wheels. When it reached dry land, the men changed gears to turn the four land wheels.

1580 A couple of horses inside this cart pushed it forward. But they could only have pushed it forward on firm, level ground. It couldn't cross plowed fields.

1795 The French were about to invade England. To defend the open beaches, Captain Adam Elliott proposed a land sloop, armed with a six-pounder gun, six muskets, and scythes on the wheels. It could travel at 6 mph (10km/h), but only if the wind was blowing!

Birth of the tank

Armored carts failed because no engine could move them fast enough and their wheels sank into the mud. Gasoline engines and caterpillar tracks solved these problems in time for World War I. When soldiers fought from trenches protected by barbed wire, it was impossible to cross the space between them without being hit. A bulletproof machine was needed that could crawl over the rough ground and crush the wire. The British were the first to design and send tanks into action in 1916.

A.D. 1770 Richard Edgeworth invented the first caterpillar track. To stop thin wheels from sinking into the mud, the weight was spread out onto wooden pads.

1854 This proposed armor-plated steam locomotive was armed with eight small cannons.

1900 This bulletproof traction engine and wagons carried soldiers and supplies during the Boer War in South Africa. It had a top speed of 10 mph (16km/h) on a good road.

1902 Fred Simms built one of the first "motor war cars." It had armor 0.25 in. (6mm) thick, a top speed of 9 mph (15km/h), and three machine guns, but the British army still wasn't interested.

1903 H. G. Wells wrote a story called "The Land Ironclads" describing huge armored vehicles running on wheels fitted with pads. They had automatic rifles and could easily cross trenches.

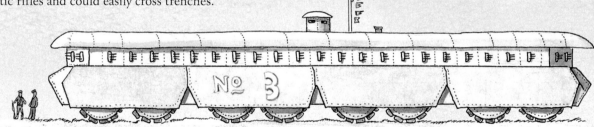

The first armored cars were fine on good roads, but they were useless traveling cross-country.

The Russian army was one of the first to buy an armored car, but no more were ordered because it frightened the horses.

1914 The British army was already using tractors running on caterpillar tracks to pull heavy guns.

1915 Soon a tractor was turned into an armored vehicle by the British. This was the very first tank, called "Little Willie."

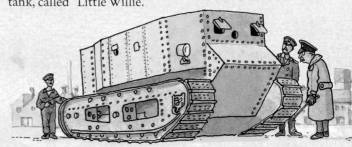

1916 The British were the first to use tanks in action. They had a gun on each side and caterpillar tracks that ran over and under the body. The spoked wheels helped them steer.

1917 Man-propelled mini tanks seemed like a good idea—on smooth ground—but the soldier's legs were dangerously exposed.

Modern tanks

When British tanks first appeared, the French and Germans quickly made their own designs. They were all crude machines that now look very strange. After the war, armies experimented with different types of tanks. Some wanted swarms of light, fast tanks; others wanted very heavy tanks. By 1939, the classic shape of the tank had evolved, with a single turret on top of an armored hull. The only difference now is that tanks have thicker armor and bigger guns.

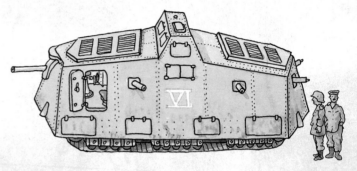

A.D. 1918 The Germans' answer to the tank was the lumbering 35-ton *Sturmpanzerwagen* with a crew of 18, six machine guns, and one small cannon. It was very slow, unable to cross ditches, and so top-heavy that it often fell over.

1917 France produced this clumsy tank weighing 24 tons and armed with a field gun and four machine guns. Its gasoline-electric engine pushed it along at a crawl. It didn't fall over, but it got its nose stuck in ditches.

1918 The French Renault light tank weighed only 7 tons and was, at 6 mph (10km/h), the fastest tank of the war. It carried two men and a small cannon in a revolving turret.

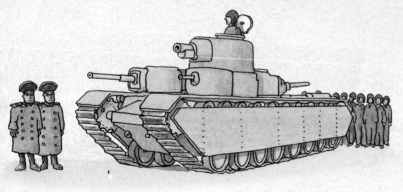

1930 This Mercedes was the first armored car. The windows were protected by steel plates that sprang up when necessary. The driver had a small vision slit; the passengers used a periscope.

1933 The Russians in the 1930s favored very heavy battle tanks. The giant T-35 weighed 55 tons, had five turrets, and held a large crew of 11 soldiers.

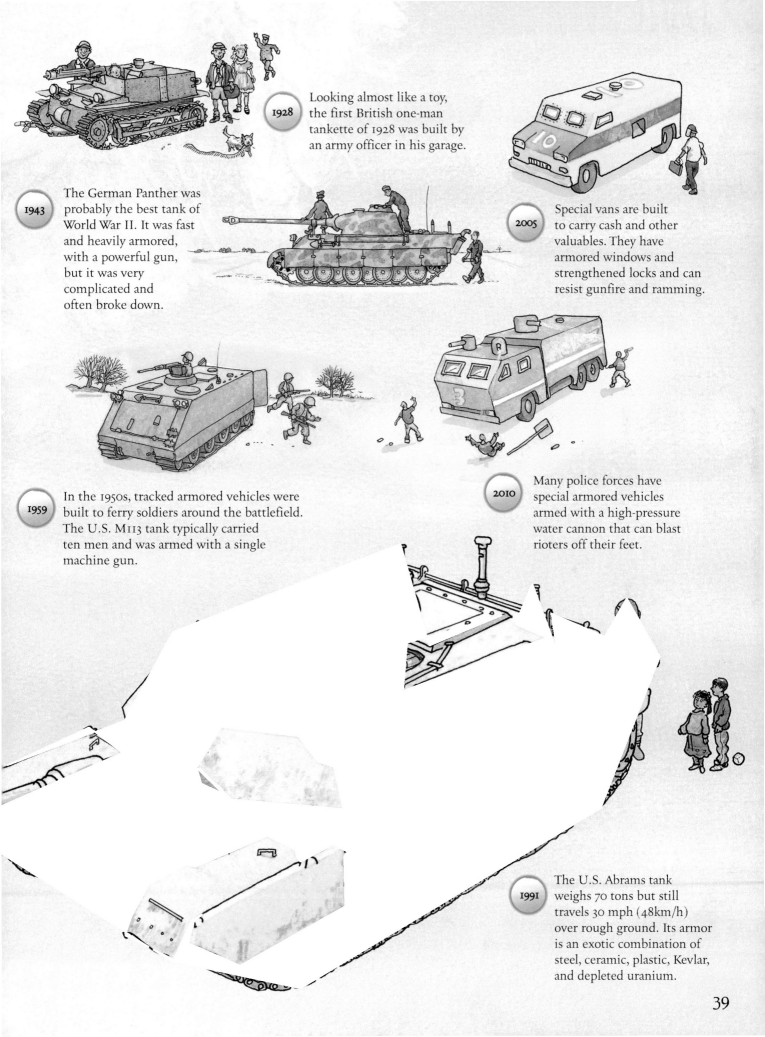

1928 Looking almost like a toy, the first British one-man tankette of 1928 was built by an army officer in his garage.

1943 The German Panther was probably the best tank of World War II. It was fast and heavily armored, with a powerful gun, but it was very complicated and often broke down.

2005 Special vans are built to carry cash and other valuables. They have armored windows and strengthened locks and can resist gunfire and ramming.

1959 In the 1950s, tracked armored vehicles were built to ferry soldiers around the battlefield. The U.S. M113 tank typically carried ten men and was armed with a single machine gun.

2010 Many police forces have special armored vehicles armed with a high-pressure water cannon that can blast rioters off their feet.

1991 The U.S. Abrams tank weighs 70 tons but still travels 30 mph (48km/h) over rough ground. Its armor is an exotic combination of steel, ceramic, plastic, Kevlar, and depleted uranium.

ARMORED TRAINS

Armored trains are at the most useful where the distances are vast and there are few roads. In such situations, the equivalent of a small, swiftly moving battleship is a powerful force. They were mainly used in South Africa during the Boer War and in Russia during the revolution and both world wars. After World War II, they became obsolete. Armored vehicles and helicopters can patrol more effectively and cannot be stopped by blowing up the rails.

1864 The Union army in the U.S. Civil War mounted a heavy gun on a railroad truck behind an armored shield. It was pushed up and down a short stretch of curved track to aim it.

1952 The British army used small gasoline-engine armored rail trolleys to patrol the railroad lines in Malaysia and protect them from the attacks of rebels.

1865 A cross section through a British armored train designed in 1865 but never built.

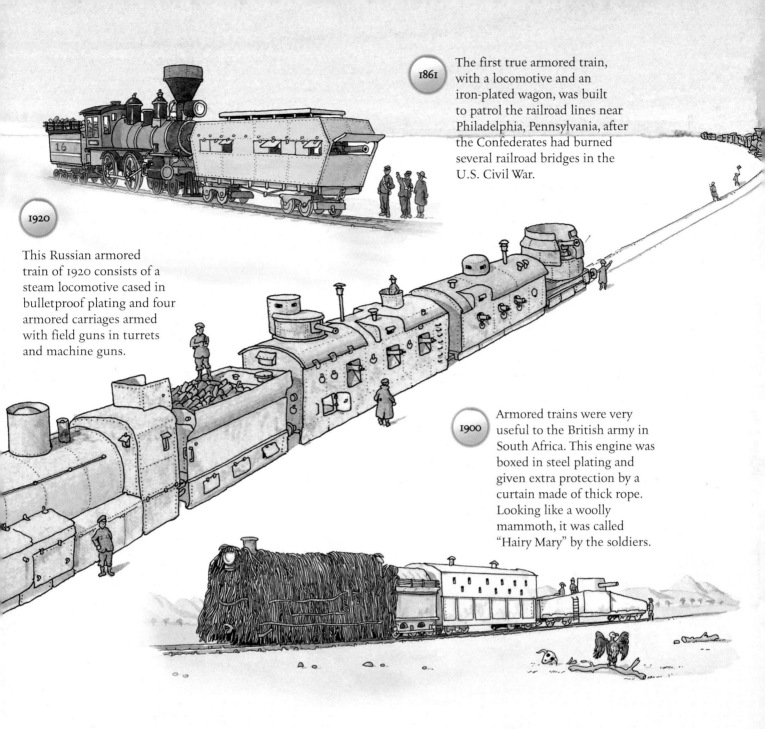

1861 The first true armored train, with a locomotive and an iron-plated wagon, was built to patrol the railroad lines near Philadelphia, Pennsylvania, after the Confederates had burned several railroad bridges in the U.S. Civil War.

1920 This Russian armored train of 1920 consists of a steam locomotive cased in bulletproof plating and four armored carriages armed with field guns in turrets and machine guns.

1900 Armored trains were very useful to the British army in South Africa. This engine was boxed in steel plating and given extra protection by a curtain made of thick rope. Looking like a woolly mammoth, it was called "Hairy Mary" by the soldiers.

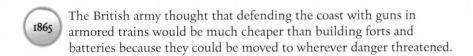

1865 The British army thought that defending the coast with guns in armored trains would be much cheaper than building forts and batteries because they could be moved to wherever danger threatened.

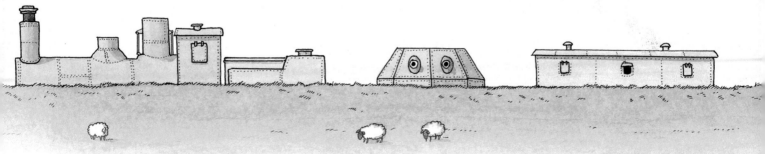

41

EARLY ARMORED SHIPS

The Romans and the Chinese sometimes put iron or brass plates on their warships, but there was no urgent need for armor until guns firing explosive shells were used in the 1840s. Shells were much more dangerous than solid cannonballs, which were usually stopped by a ship's thick timbers. The solution was to attach iron plates to the hull, and the new warships built in the second half of the 1800s became known as "ironclads." They were too heavy to use sail power alone, and they all had steam engines.

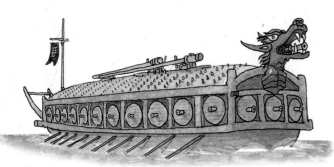

1592 The Koreans built several turtle ships to fight against the Japanese. The spiked iron roof protected the crew from arrows and bullets and, most important, made the ship impossible to board.

1483 This fanciful floating fortress was originally drawn in 1483. The crew members are armed with spears, halberds, crossbows, and primitive handguns. As they are all wearing armor, they must be very confident that the ship will not be sunk.

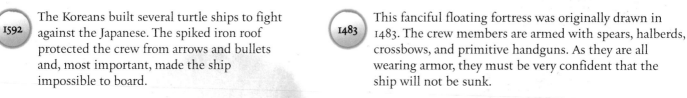

1859 France launched the first seagoing armored ship in 1859, called the *Gloire*. She was 256 ft. (78m) long and weighed 6,200 tons. Her armor was 4.8 in. (121mm) thick, and she was armed with 36 guns.

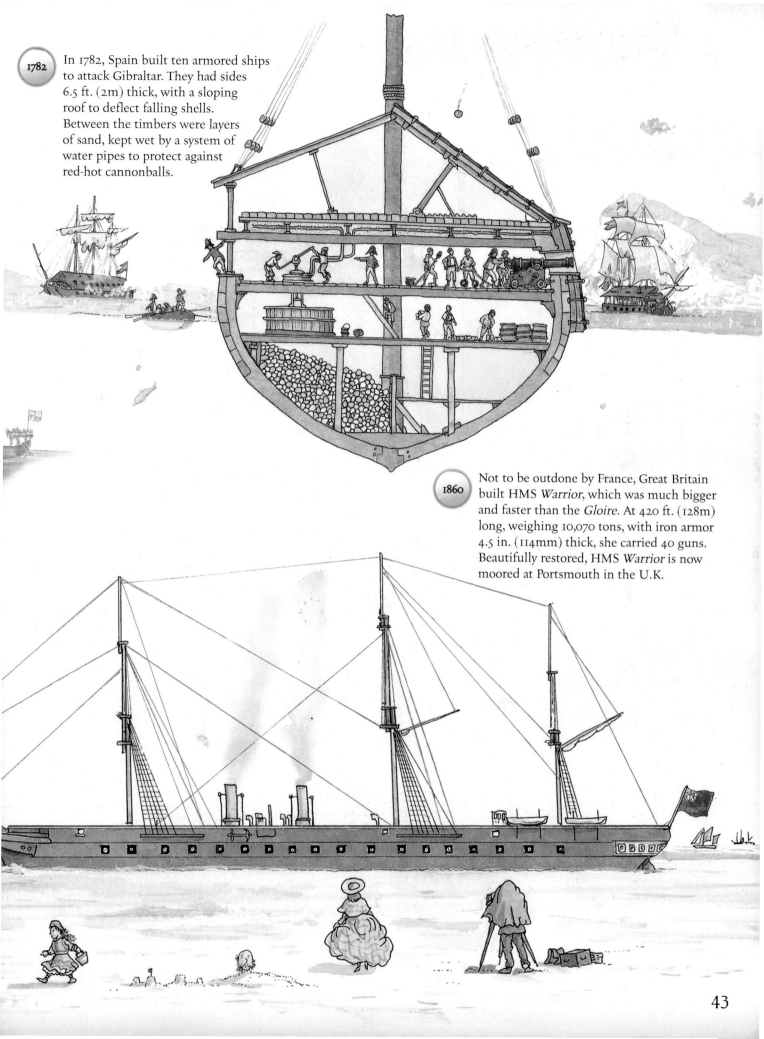

1782 In 1782, Spain built ten armored ships to attack Gibraltar. They had sides 6.5 ft. (2m) thick, with a sloping roof to deflect falling shells. Between the timbers were layers of sand, kept wet by a system of water pipes to protect against red-hot cannonballs.

1860 Not to be outdone by France, Great Britain built HMS *Warrior*, which was much bigger and faster than the *Gloire*. At 420 ft. (128m) long, weighing 10,070 tons, with iron armor 4.5 in. (114mm) thick, she carried 40 guns. Beautifully restored, HMS *Warrior* is now moored at Portsmouth in the U.K.

43

BATTLE OF THE IRONCLADS: U.S.S. MONITOR VS. C.S.S. VIRGINIA

When the U.S. Civil War began, the Union navy blockaded the Confederate coast to stop them from getting supplies. The Confederates decided to build an armored ship to destroy the wooden Union ships. They took the hull of a frigate, renamed her *Virginia*, and cut the sides down to within 1.5 ft. (0.5m) of the water. On the deck, they built a casemate (an armored enclosure for guns) with thick, sloping wooden sides covered with iron plates.

The next day, the *Virginia* sailed out to finish off the rest of the Union fleet, only to be met by another, even stranger ship. Looking like a "cheese box on a plank," the U.S.S. *Monitor* was truly revolutionary: the first ship to mount guns in a revolving turret. The historic first battle between armored ships lasted for four hours. The *Virginia* was hit 41 times and the *Monitor* 21, but neither ship could harm the other. The fight was a draw, but the overall battle was a victory for the *Monitor* because she saved the rest of the fleet.

On March 7, 1862, the *Virginia* steamed into the natural harbor of Hampton Roads. The Union ships fired furiously, but their shot and shell bounced off the *Virginia* as she slowly advanced to sink two warships and force another aground.

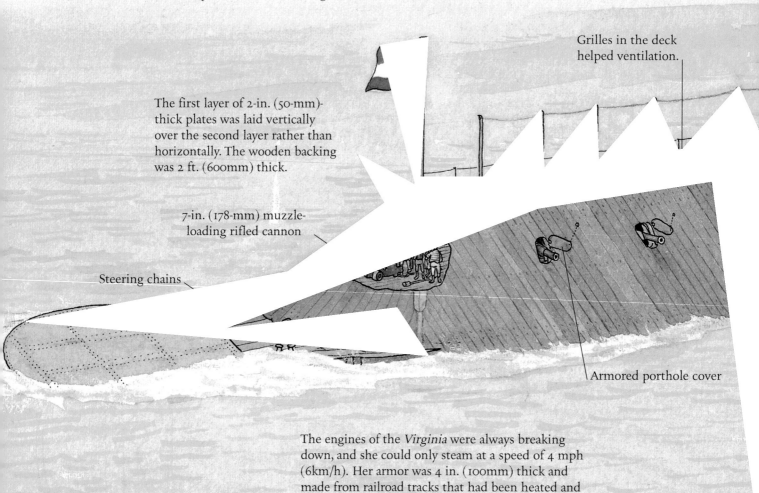

Grilles in the deck helped ventilation.

The first layer of 2-in. (50-mm)-thick plates was laid vertically over the second layer rather than horizontally. The wooden backing was 2 ft. (600mm) thick.

7-in. (178-mm) muzzle-loading rifled cannon

Steering chains

Armored porthole cover

The engines of the *Virginia* were always breaking down, and she could only steam at a speed of 4 mph (6km/h). Her armor was 4 in. (100mm) thick and made from railroad tracks that had been heated and rolled into plates.

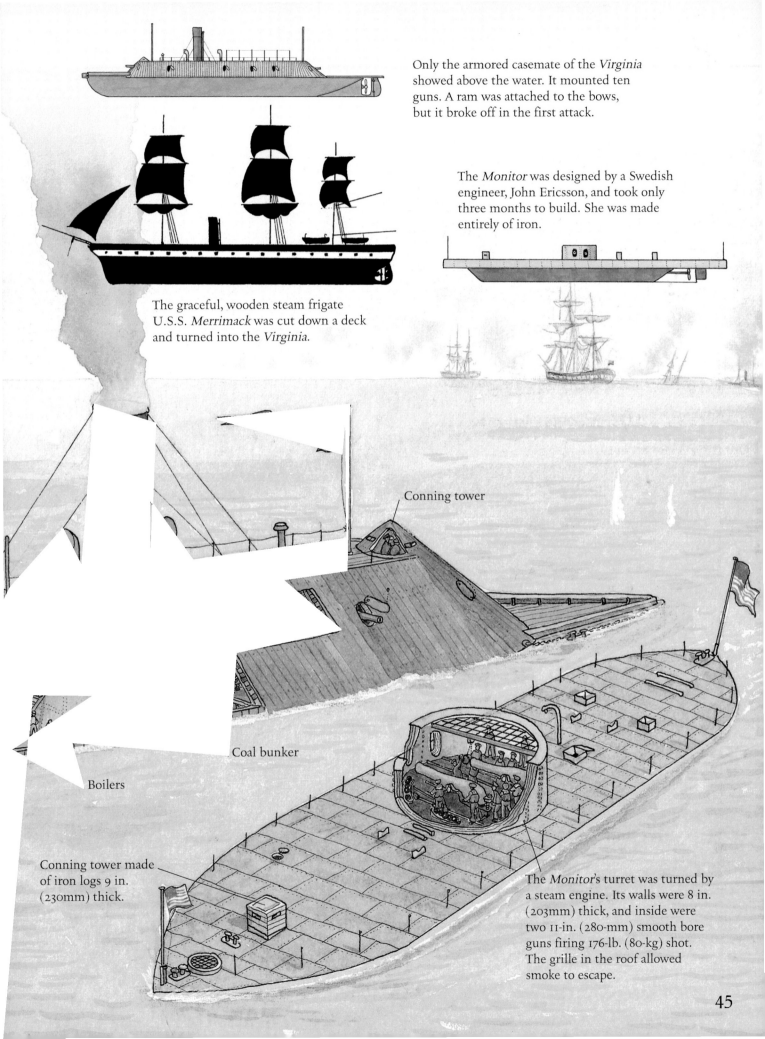

Only the armored casemate of the *Virginia* showed above the water. It mounted ten guns. A ram was attached to the bows, but it broke off in the first attack.

The *Monitor* was designed by a Swedish engineer, John Ericsson, and took only three months to build. She was made entirely of iron.

The graceful, wooden steam frigate U.S.S. *Merrimack* was cut down a deck and turned into the *Virginia*.

Conning tower

Coal bunker

Boilers

Conning tower made of iron logs 9 in. (230mm) thick.

The *Monitor*'s turret was turned by a steam engine. Its walls were 8 in. (203mm) thick, and inside were two 11-in. (280-mm) smooth bore guns firing 176-lb. (80-kg) shot. The grille in the roof allowed smoke to escape.

45

MODERN BATTLESHIPS

The first ironclads mounted their guns in rows along the sides or in turrets. It was not obvious which way was the best. The rest of the 1800s was a time of experimentation, and many strange designs were tried out until the turret was accepted. Although all battleships were powered by steam, most carried sails until the 1890s. The classic modern battleship of the 1900s carried enormous guns in three or four turrets, with armor up to 16 in. (400mm) thick.

165 ft. (50m)

1865
The turret ship *Huascar* was built in Great Britain for Peru. She was captured by Chile in 1879 and still survives as a museum ship.

1867
The German *Kronprinz* was a typical broadside ironclad of the 1860s, with sails and a ramming bow. She had armor 5 in. (127mm) thick and carried 16 guns.

1872

The British Royal Navy's *Thunderer* was the first battleship without sails. She carried four 12-in. (305-mm) guns in two turrets. There was a terrible accident aboard when a gun was loaded twice by mistake and exploded.

165 ft. (50m)

165 ft. (50m)

1944
U.S.S. *Missouri*, 1944, was the fastest battleship ever, with a speed of 38 mph (61km/h). She carried nine 16-in. (406-mm) guns and last saw action in the first Gulf War in 1991 before retiring the following year.

165 ft. (50m)

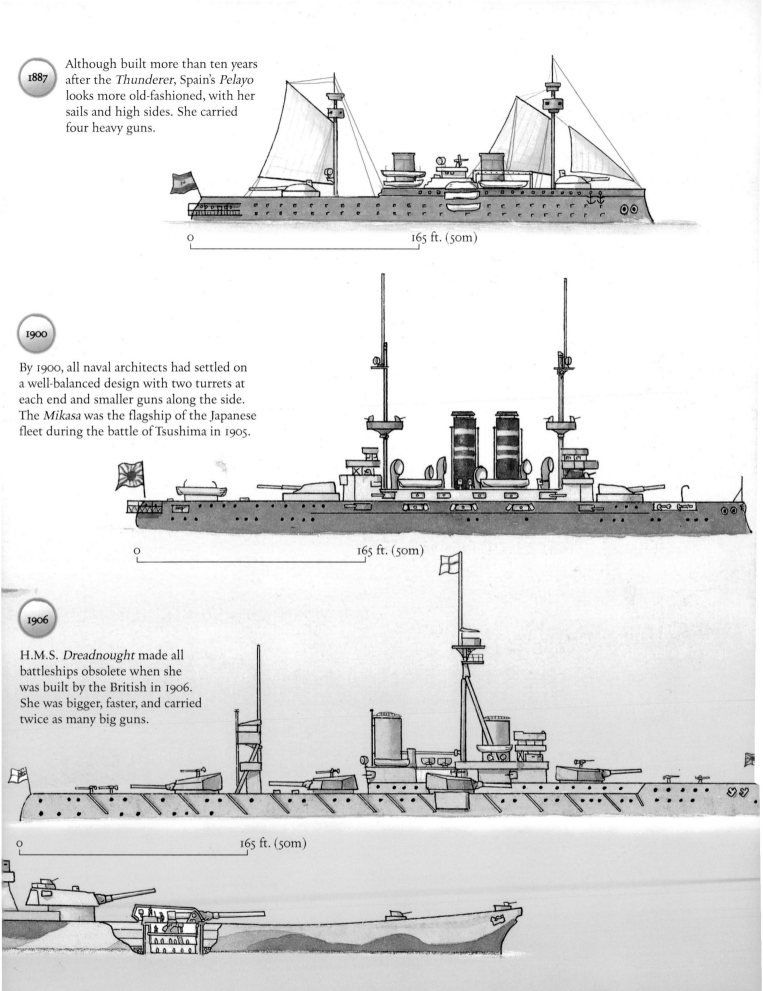

1887 Although built more than ten years after the *Thunderer*, Spain's *Pelayo* looks more old-fashioned, with her sails and high sides. She carried four heavy guns.

0   165 ft. (50m)

1900 By 1900, all naval architects had settled on a well-balanced design with two turrets at each end and smaller guns along the side. The *Mikasa* was the flagship of the Japanese fleet during the battle of Tsushima in 1905.

0   165 ft. (50m)

1906 H.M.S. *Dreadnought* made all battleships obsolete when she was built by the British in 1906. She was bigger, faster, and carried twice as many big guns.

0   165 ft. (50m)

47

DEEP-SEA DIVING VESSELS

Some of the most heavily armored ships are not protected against the sudden blow from a shell but instead from the slow, steady, terrible crushing pressure of the depths of the sea. Water is very heavy, and the deeper an object sinks, the greater the pressure is on it. Thousands of feet down, tons press on every square inch. A vessel designed to explore the still-mysterious ocean depths has to be incredibly strong.

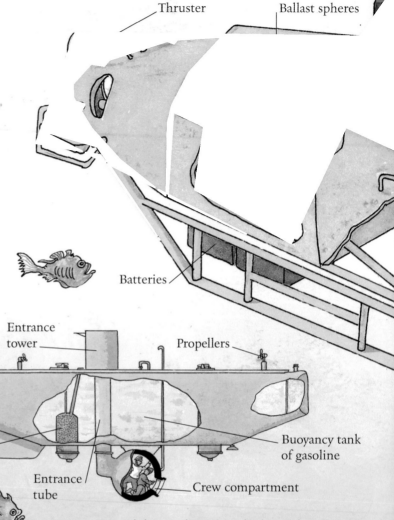

Thruster   Ballast spheres

Batteries

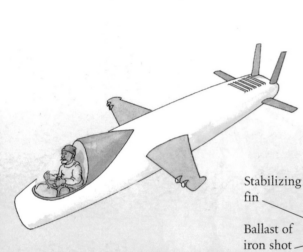

The very latest deep-diving craft are designed to be very mobile, "flying" through the water on stubby wings. The cockpit is made of very tough plastic—strong enough to resist the pressure at 980 ft. (300m).

Entrance tower

Propellers

Stabilizing fin

Ballast of iron shot

Entrance tube

Crew compartment

Buoyancy tank of gasoline

Auguste Piccard designed *Trieste*, a bathyscaphe (Greek for "deep ship") that floated, rising to the surface without the need for a heavy cable and with propellers so that it could move.

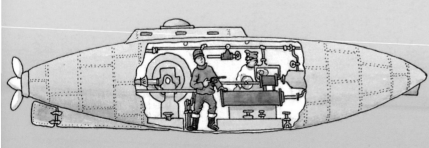

A submarine is safe as long as it doesn't go below its designated safe depth. That depth depends on the strength of the hull.

As the submarine sinks deeper, the pressure increases and, once beyond the safe limit, something will give way and water will cascade in. But once the submarine is full of water, the pressure will equalize and, however deep it sinks, it will not be squashed any more.

Entry hatch

In 1965, a new deep-sea vehicle was launched that could dive to 13,120 ft. (4,000m). *Alvin* had a neat hull filled with high-pressure ballast spheres instead of a tank of gasoline.

Sonar

Camera

Strobe lights

Sample basket

Sphere with room for crew of three

Manipulators

This strange-looking submarine tank was lowered down to the depths and then cast off its cable to crawl around.

Chemical apparatus to remove carbon dioxide

Wooden skids

In 1932, a famous naturalist, William Beebe, and a young engineer, Otis Barton, built an armored globe that they called a bathysphere. Beebe and Barton made more than a dozen dives and, in 1934, reached a depth of 3,028 ft. (923m), farther down than any living man had ever gone.

Cable containing electrical power and telephone wire

Oxygen tank

The bathysphere was made from a single casting of iron, with walls 18 in. (450mm) thick. There were two windows made of quartz, the only transparent material able to resist the immense pressure. The bathysphere was attached to a winch aboard its mother ship by 3,510 ft. (1,070m) of steel cable.

49

ARMORED PLANES

During World War I, aircraft started flying low to attack targets on the ground. Many were shot down, so designers produced rugged metal planes fitted with armor. Many fighters in World War II had armor around the cockpit, and bombers had armored seats for the pilots. Today, jets fly so fast that armor is unnecessary except for ground-attack aircraft. The danger to passenger planes is more often from inside. Flight-deck doors have strong locks, and strengthened luggage containers lessen the damage caused by a bomb smuggled inside a suitcase.

1918 The German Junkers J-4 was the first all-metal biplane. The crew, engine, and gasoline tank were all protected by sheets of 0.2-in. (5-mm) armor.

1941 The Russian Stormovik's nickname was "The Flying Tank" because it was so heavily armored. It flew close to the ground and destroyed thousands of German vehicles during World War II.

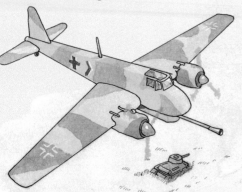

1942 The windshield of the German Henschel Hs 129 was 3 in. (75mm) thick, and the cockpit was armor-plated. Its huge 3-in. (75-mm) gun was deadly to Russian tanks.

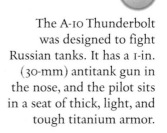

1974 The A-10 Thunderbolt was designed to fight Russian tanks. It has a 1-in. (30-mm) antitank gun in the nose, and the pilot sits in a seat of thick, light, and tough titanium armor.

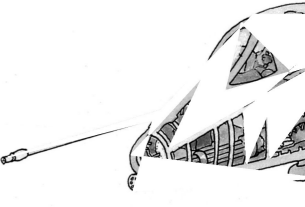

2010 Attack and troop-carrying helicopters have to fly low and slowly over the battlefield, so they are protected around the cockpit and engine with lightweight plastic and ceramic armor.

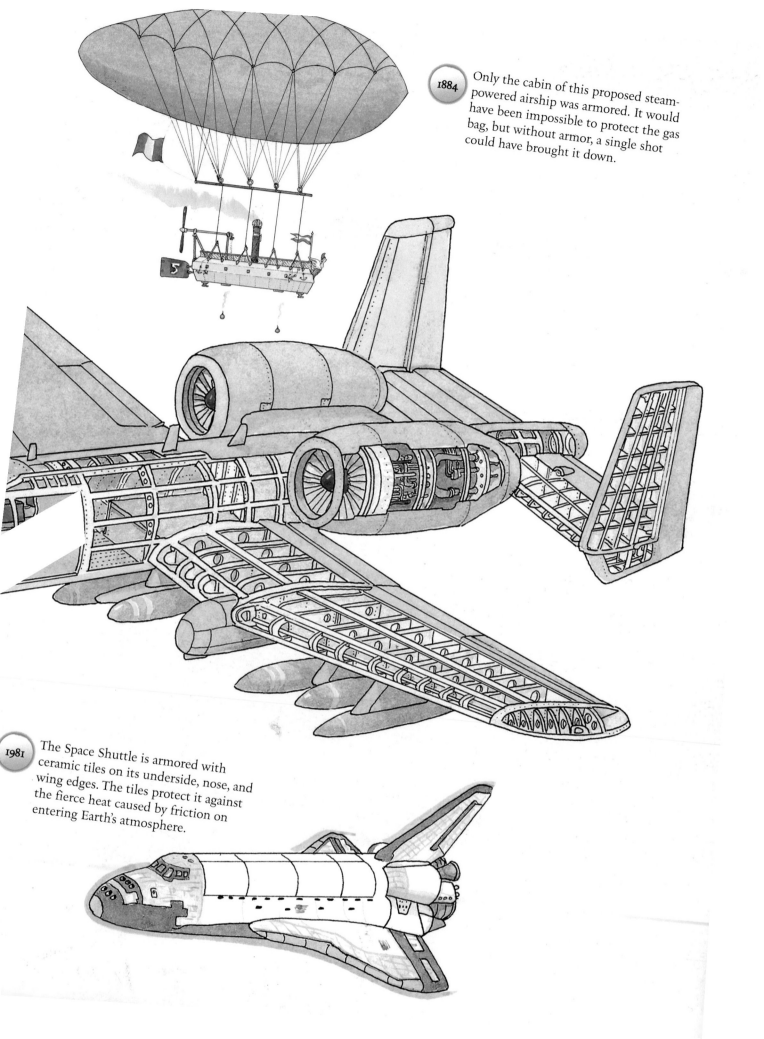

1884 Only the cabin of this proposed steam-powered airship was armored. It would have been impossible to protect the gas bag, but without armor, a single shot could have brought it down.

1981 The Space Shuttle is armored with ceramic tiles on its underside, nose, and wing edges. The tiles protect it against the fierce heat caused by friction on entering Earth's atmosphere.

ARMORED BUILDINGS

Doors and windows are the weakest points in any building. Since early times, doors have been strengthened with bolts and windows covered by bars. In modern cities, many homes and offices have security grilles over their doors and windows. Some have armored shutters and even bulletproof windows. The Oval Office of the U.S. president has windows able to withstand a small missile.

This medieval door has its thick timbers bound with iron straps. A tiny barred window allows the doorkeeper to see who's knocking.

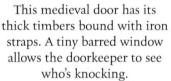

In warm countries, downstairs windows were covered by iron grilles so the house could be open to the air but not to robbers or, in this picture, would-be suitors.

The strongest and heaviest doors are found in bank vaults, safes, and strongrooms. Designed to resist attacks by explosives and heat cutters, they have very complicated locks.

The "Impregnable Iron Fortress," designed in England in 1860, had walls of iron blocks dovetailed together with portholes for 70 cannons. Three were proposed to guard the Thames estuary in London, England, but were never built.

Some German forts were built with walls made from large iron plates. They were put together like giant pieces of ready-to-assemble furniture.

IRON ISLAND

This extraordinary iron fort sits in the sea a couple of miles away from Portsmouth, England. It cost a fortune, took almost 20 years to finish, and never fired its guns at an enemy. So why was it built?

More than 150 years ago, cannons had a very short range. They could not hit anything farther away than 0.6 mi. (1km). This was a big problem for the British army, who wanted to defend the approach to Portsmouth, which was Great Britain's most important naval base.

The distance from Portsmouth to the Isle of Wight, across the stretch of water called the Solent, was almost 4 mi. (6.5km). Any ship sailing down the middle of the Solent would be relatively safe; no gun on land could hit it. If only there was another island in the Solent, dreamed the army. Then, ingenious Victorian engineers solved the problem and built artificial islands in the sea with a fort on each one. Work started in 1861.

Crane for lifting supplies

Winch

Small crane

Landing stage

This Russian fort was built in 1897 to protect the entrance to Saint Petersburg harbor. The front wall is made of iron plate.

In 1940, Great Britain feared invasion by the German army from across the English Channel, and thousands of concrete pillboxes and gun batteries were quickly built. A cheap alternative was this small steel turret. Its machine gun could fire from the roof against aircraft or from the front against troops and tanks.

During World War II, railroad workers and sentries were often caught outside in an air raid and needed to find shelter quickly. Steel one-man shelters like this were quick and simple to install and could be moved easily. Anyone inside was safe from everything except a direct hit.

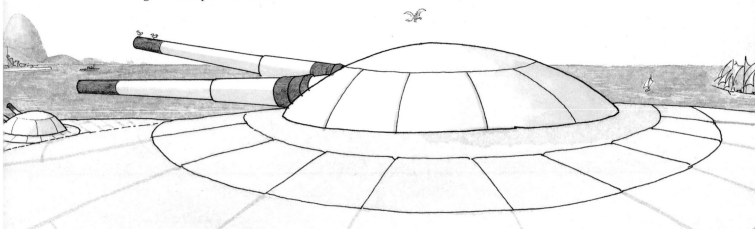

Fort Copacabana was built in 1914 to defend the entrance to Rio de Janeiro harbor, in Brazil. All that can be seen is the concrete roof and two gun turrets.

The biggest of the forts was called No Man's Land. It was completely circular and armed with 49 heavy guns. The bottom floors were made of hard granite, but the top two stories were built of iron. The outside wall was a sandwich of armor plate and especially hard iron concrete 16 in. (400mm) thick. The fort's skin weighed 2,750 tons, probably the heaviest suit of armor ever made. It was probably also the most expensive: the fort cost the enormous sum (in those days) of around £500,000 (about $750,000).

It was painted in a checkered pattern of black and yellow squares, with a lighthouse on top to warn ships. The fort had its own bakery and fresh water from a well. The garrison of 300 soldiers exercised by running around the roof, swimming, and hauling the heavy shells to the guns.

But almost as soon as the fort was finished, new guns were invented that could fire up to 10 mi. (16km), and No Man's Land was rendered useless.

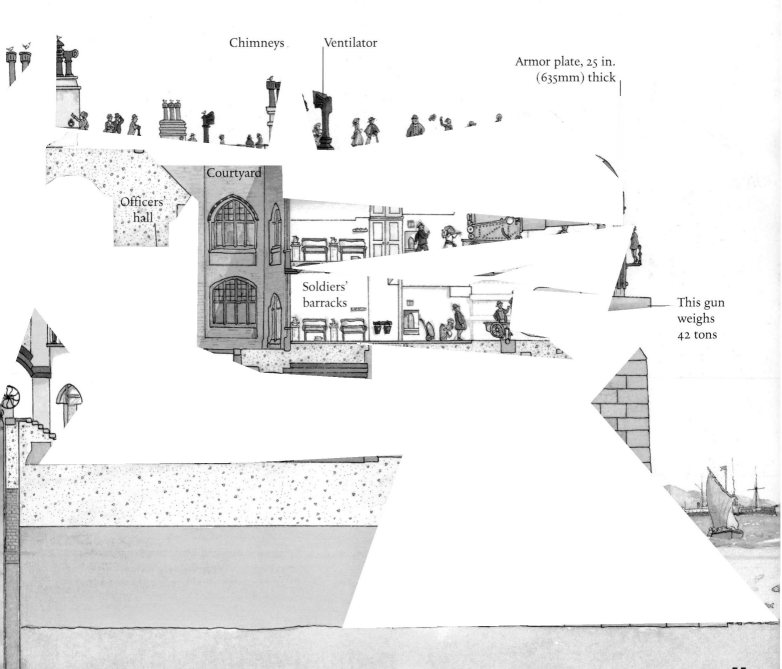

Chimneys

Ventilator

Armor plate, 25 in. (635mm) thick

Courtyard

Officers' hall

Soldiers' barracks

This gun weighs 42 tons

FORTS ON LAND

In the late 1800s, guns firing high-explosive shells forced a redesign of all forts on land. The new underground forts were made of concrete and covered with soil. All the guns were in armored turrets that could fire in any direction, so a fort needed fewer guns to cover the same area and the guns were completely protected. All that could be seen from a distance was a low mound with a few metal domes showing above the grass.

In the 1930s, France built a chain of forts called the Maginot Line to defend its border with Germany. All that was visible aboveground were gun turrets that popped up to fire and steel lookout and machine-gun turrets like this. Underneath was virtually a small town, with storage areas, barracks, a power station, and even an underground railway.

Switzerland had many forts with armored turrets in the Alps, guarding roads and railroad lines until the 1990s. They were often disguised in ingenious ways. Inside this cowshed is a turret with a heavy gun.

During World War II, the Japanese used small steel pillboxes to defend islands in the Pacific Ocean. They were light enough to be moved to wherever they were needed.

Mobile armored turrets were used in the fortifications of Romania. The wheels were used only to move the turrets to a prepared position.

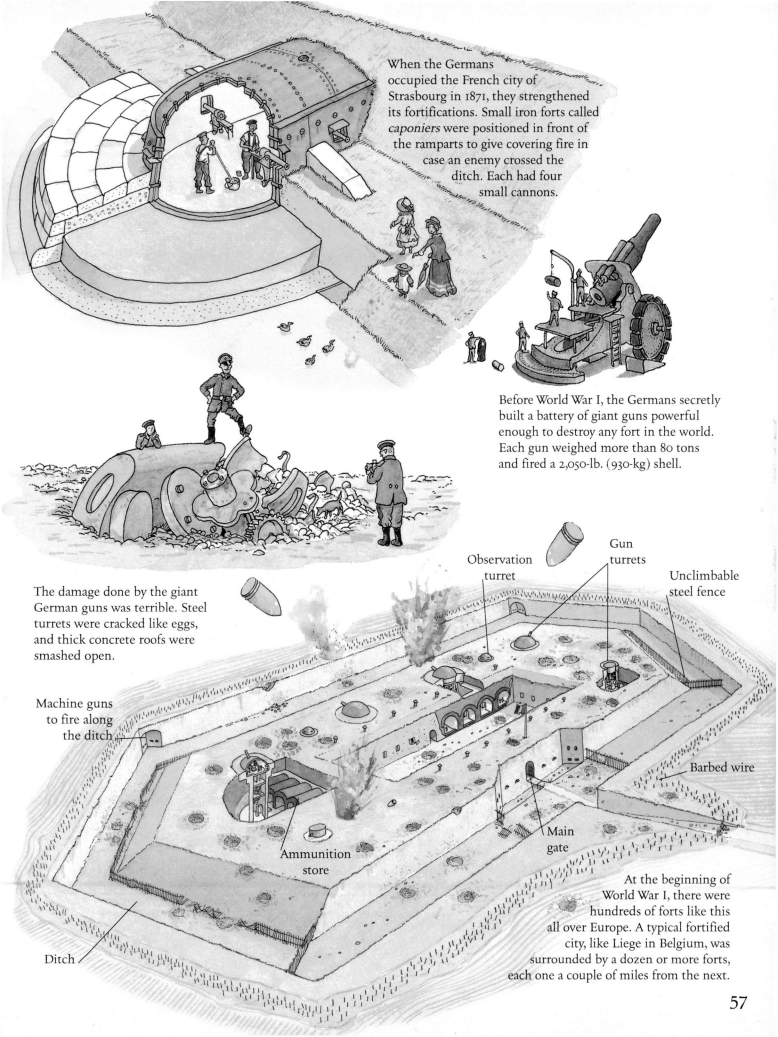

When the Germans occupied the French city of Strasbourg in 1871, they strengthened its fortifications. Small iron forts called *caponiers* were positioned in front of the ramparts to give covering fire in case an enemy crossed the ditch. Each had four small cannons.

Before World War I, the Germans secretly built a battery of giant guns powerful enough to destroy any fort in the world. Each gun weighed more than 80 tons and fired a 2,050-lb. (930-kg) shell.

The damage done by the giant German guns was terrible. Steel turrets were cracked like eggs, and thick concrete roofs were smashed open.

Observation turret

Gun turrets

Unclimbable steel fence

Machine guns to fire along the ditch

Barbed wire

Ammunition store

Main gate

Ditch

At the beginning of World War I, there were hundreds of forts like this all over Europe. A typical fortified city, like Liege in Belgium, was surrounded by a dozen or more forts, each one a couple of miles from the next.

57

Magic armor

Every warrior's dream was for some magic defense—an invisible layer that would deflect arrows and sword cuts and make him invincible. That kind of magic exists only in legends of gods and heroes, but soldiers have always gone into battle hoping to be kept safe by heavenly means as well as earthly. Spells and prayers have always been recited over armor to give it extra strength, and even today, priests sprinkle modern battle tanks with holy water.

Most armor was blessed during the Middle Ages. Some armor had a holy relic attached to it in the pious hope that the saints would make extra efforts to protect the wearer.

When Achilles, the Greek hero of the Trojan Wars, was a baby, his mother dipped him into the magic waters of the River Styx so that no weapon could ever harm him. Unfortunately, she forgot about his heel, which she held as she dunked him in the water. It was in this spot that he was later hit by an arrow and killed.

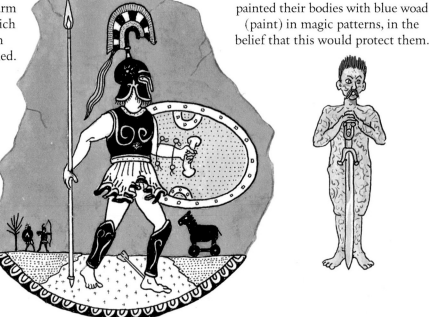

Some Celtic warriors fought naked to show how brave they were. They painted their bodies with blue woad (paint) in magic patterns, in the belief that this would protect them.

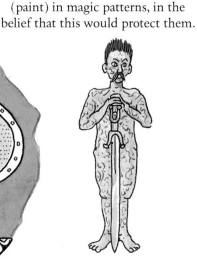

Native-American warriors who had taken part in a special religious ceremony—the Ghost Dance—wore a buckskin shirt decorated with magic symbols. Unfortunately for them, it was no use at all against the bullets of the U.S. cavalry.

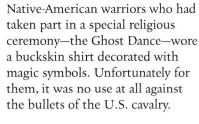

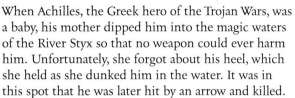

Dervishes, the followers of the Mahdi (a spiritual leader) in the Sudan, wore quilted cotton robes called *jibbas*. They believed that the special cotton patches and their faith would keep them safe from bullets—but they were wrong.

PRIVATE ARMOR

Armor is not just for soldiers. Anybody who feels in danger wants to be protected, but steel armor is too heavy and can't be worn with ordinary clothes. Bulletproof vests made out of silk and cotton were developed in the late 1800s and were surprisingly effective. Politicians and royalty who feared assassination were eager to buy them.

John Bradshaw, the judge at the trial of King Charles I of England, was so scared of being shot by an angry royalist that he wore a hat reinforced with iron and a breastplate under his robes.

Ned Kelly and his gang of Australian bandits wore suits of armor made from plow blades. They were bulletproof but did not cover the legs, so that was where the police shot Kelly.

The 1920s were a violent time in some U.S. cities. Gangsters and private detectives were the best customers for bulletproof vests.

These stylish steel glasses were on sale at the beginning of World War II.

As the threat of war loomed in 1938, this armored, gas-proof baby buggy went on sale. Very few were bought because, unsurprisingly, nobody wanted to take their baby out during an air raid.

Moms worried about the threat of drive-by shootings on the mean streets can keep their baby safe in this armored stroller, guaranteed against machine-gun bullets.

GLOSSARY

amphibious Having the ability to move equally well on land and water. Amphibious vehicles have been around since the 1500s.

Assyria A fierce and warlike power that dominated the Middle East from 900 to 600 B.C.

ball-and-socket joint A flexible joint formed by one part ending in a ball and the other in a curved socket to hold the ball. A natural version of this is where the leg joins the hip.

brass A metal made by mixing copper with zinc. Copper is a very soft metal, and zinc makes it harder.

breech loading Loading a gun from the breech, or opposite end from the muzzle. This method is easier, faster, and safer than muzzle loading.

bronze A metal made from copper and tin.

cast iron When iron melts, it can be formed or cast into almost any shape by being poured into a mold.

ceramic A material made from nonmetallic elements by the application of heat, such as a tile, brick, or pot. Ceramic plates can be very strong and are lighter than metal ones.

Confederate In 1861, the 11 Southern states of the U.S. split from the Northern states to form their own country, which they called the Confederate States of America (aka the Confederacy). This led to a civil war between the Confederates and the remaining states, who were known as the Federals, or the Union. The Confederates were defeated in 1865 and rejoined the U.S.

cuirass Armor protecting the upper body, consisting of a breastplate and backplate.

cuirassier A cavalryman wearing a cuirass and helmet.

cupola A small, rounded dome on a fort used either for observation or to protect guns.

Dayak A group of tribes who live by the rivers in Borneo and Sarawak, in Malaysia. They used to be famous for headhunting.

depleted uranium A very dense metal—almost twice as heavy as lead—that is used to make armor and bullets.

fiberglass A metal made from glass spun into fine threads. Mixed with plastic resin, it makes a strong material that is easily molded into shape.

gauntlet A heavy glove of leather or steel.

halberd A fearsome weapon with a combined ax blade, spear, and hook mounted on the end of a long pole.

Hittite The name for the fierce and warlike people who were the dominant power from 1750 to 1200 B.C. in what is now Turkey.

Hussites The followers of the religious leader Jan Huss (c. 1369–1415) in what is now the Czech Republic. They wanted their own national church and fought for many years against the armies of the German emperor, who wanted to make them part of the Roman Catholic Church.

ironclad The first armored ships were actually wooden ships with an outer layer of iron plate, hence the name "ironclad." Later, all armored ships were called ironclads, even though they were built of, and armored with, steel.

Kevlar A very strong synthetic material made from spun plastic fibers. It is woven into sheets to make modern body armor and protective clothing.

loophole A narrow slit window in a castle or fort from which bows or guns are fired.

muzzle The dangerous end of a gun from which the bullet emerges.

muzzle loading Loading a cannon from the end of the muzzle. This is always a slower process than breech loading and is more dangerous.

pike A very long spear.

red-hot shot Solid cannonballs heated in a furnace and then fired at wooden ships to set them ablaze.

rifled cannon A cannon with twisting grooves cut inside the barrel. These spin the shell as it is fired to make it go farther and with greater accuracy.

rubberized Describes materials such as cloth or canvas that have been treated with a rubber solution to make them waterproof.

shell A projectile filled with an explosive. At first, shells were round like solid cannonballs, but those fired from rifled cannons were cylinders with a pointed end.

sloop A small sailing ship with a single mast.

smooth bore A cannon with no grooves inside the barrel.

sonar SOund Navigation And Ranging—a machine that sends out sound waves to measure the depth of water or to detect obstacles and other vessels.

steel An alloy or mixture of mostly iron, with a tiny amount of carbon to add strength. It is much stronger and more flexible than pure iron.

strobe A very bright light flashing at a regular frequency.

Sumerian Sumer was the first civilization in which people lived in cities. It flourished in Mesopotamia (now modern Iraq) from around 3000 to 1900 B.C.

synthetic An artificial material made by putting together separate elements. Rubber is a natural material produced by trees, but synthetic rubber can be made from chemicals.

titanium A metal that is much stronger than steel but weighs only half as much.

Union During the U.S. Civil War, the Northern states were known as the Union because they were still part of the United States of America.

visor The movable part of a helmet covering the face.

wrought iron Iron is wrought when it is hammered into shape while red-hot (think of a blacksmith shaping a horseshoe) rather than melted and poured into a mold.

FURTHER INFORMATION

Where to see armor

Many museums have small collections of armor, but those listed here are some of the very best from around the world, with beautiful examples of the armorers' skill. Many museums hold events with mock fights and tournaments, and some even let you try on the armor.

Austria
The Armoury of the State of Styria, Graz (www.zeughaus.at)
Art History Museum, Vienna (www.khm.at)

Belgium
Army and Military History Museum, Brussels (www.klm-mra.be)

Canada
The Royal Ontario Museum, Toronto (www.rom.on.ca)

Denmark
The Royal Arsenal Museum, Copenhagen (www.thm.dk)

France
Army Museum, Les Invalides, Paris (www.invalides.org)

Germany
The Baden State Museum, Karlsruhe (www.landesmuseum.de/website)
The Bavarian National Museum, Munich (www.bayerisches-nationalmuseum.de)
The Bavarian Army Museum, Ingoldstadt (www.bayerisches-armeemuseum.de)
The Imperial Castle, Nuremberg (www.schloesser.bayern.de/englisch/palace/objects/nbg_burg.htm)

Italy
Churburg Castle, Churburg (www.churburg.com/willkommen_engl/index.html)
Bargello, Florence (www.polomuseale.firenze.it/english/musei/bargello)
Royal Armoury, Turin (www.artito.arti.beniculturali.it/Armeria%20Reale/DefaultArmeria.htm)

Japan
National Museum, Tokyo (www.tnm.go.jp)

The Netherlands
Army Museum, Delft (www.armymuseum.nl)

Russia
Kremlin Museum, Moscow (www.kreml.ru/en/main/museums/)
State Hermitage Museum, Saint Petersburg (www.hermitagemuseum.org)

Spain
Royal Armoury, Madrid (www.patrimonionacional.es/Home/Palacios-Reales/Palacio-Real-de-Madrid.aspx)

Sweden
The Royal Armoury, Stockholm (www.livrustkammaren.se)

Switzerland
National Museum, Zurich (www.musee-suisse.com)
Museum of History, Berne (www.bhm.ch)

United Kingdom
Fitzwilliam Museum, Cambridge (www.fitzmuseum.cam.ac.uk)
Art Gallery and Museum, Glasgow (www.glasgowmuseums.com)
Royal Armouries, Leeds (www.royalarmouries.org)
British Museum, London (www.britishmuseum.org/default.aspx)
National Army Museum, London (www.national-army-museum.ac.uk)
Tower of London, London (www.hrp.org.uk/TowerOfLondon)
The Wallace Collection, London (www.wallacecollection.org)
Victoria and Albert Museum, London (www.vam.ac.uk)
Warwick Castle, Warwick (www.warwick-castle.co.uk)

United States
The Art Institute of Chicago, Chicago, IL (www.artic.edu/aic)
Museum of Art, Cleveland, OH (www.clemusart.com)
Metropolitan Museum of Art, New York, NY (www.metmuseum.org)
The Higgins Armory Museum, Worcester, MA (www.higgins.org)

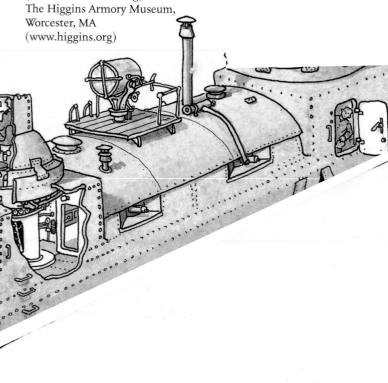